Every Kid's Guide to

Laws that Relate to Kids in the Community

Written by
JOY BERRY

CHILDRENS PRESS ®
CHICAGO

About the Author and Publisher

Joy Berry's mission in life is to help families cope with everyday problems and to help children become competent, responsible, happy individuals. To achieve her goal, she has written over two hundred self-help books for children from infancy through age twelve. Her work has revolutionized children's publishing by providing families with practical, how-to, living skills information that was previously unavailable in children's books.

Joy has gathered a dedicated team of experts, including psychologists, educators, child developmentalists, writers, editors, designers, and artists to form her publishing company and to help produce her work.

The company, Living Skills Press, produces thoroughly researched books and audiovisual materials that successfully combine humor and education to teach children subjects ranging from how to clean a bedroom to how to resolve problems and get along with other people.

Managing Editor: Ellen Klarberg
Copy Editors: Kate Dickey, Annette Gooch
Contributing Editors: Jean Buckley, Nancy Cochran, Barbara Detrich, Frank Elia, Bob Gillen, Kathleen McBride, Susan Motycka, Gary Passarino
Editorial Assistant: Sandy Passarino

Art Director: Laurie Westdahl
Design: Abigail Johnston, Laurie Westdahl
Production: Abigail Johnston, Caroline Rennard
Illustrations designed by: Bartholomew
Inker: Susie Hornig
Colorer: Susie Hornig
Composition: Curt Chelin

There are special laws that apply to children.

In **EVERY KID'S GUIDE TO LAWS THAT RELATE TO KIDS IN THE COMMUNITY,** you will learn the following:

- what some legal words mean,
- what torts are,
- what crimes are, and
- what laws protect children.

BECAUSE YOU ARE CHILDREN, THERE ARE SPECIAL LAWS THAT APPLY TO YOU.
ARE THERE LAWS FOR DOGS?

Before you can understand the laws that apply to you, it will help to know the meaning of certain legal words.

One definition of the word ***legal*** is "having to do with the law." Therefore, legal words are words that have to do with law.

OOPS!
... AND THAT'S ONE DEFINITION OF LEGAL.
I WONDER IF IT'S LEGAL TO SUE SOMEONE FOR CUPCAKE ASSAULT.

The word ***legal*** has a second definition. Legal also means "allowed by the law" or "lawful." If something is legal, it is OK to do.

In accordance with means "in agreement with." When you do something that is in accordance with the law, you go along with the law. You obey it and do what it tells you to do.

IT'S LEGAL FOR YOU TO CROSS THE STREET IF YOU USE THE CROSSWALK. USING THE CROSSWALK IS IN ACCORDANCE WITH THE LAW.
WALK
STOP
I'M GOOD AT OBEYING!

Illegal means "not allowed by law" or "unlawful." If something is illegal, it is *not* OK to do.

Against means "in opposition to." When you go against the law, you oppose the law. You disobey it and do not do what it tells you to do.

In violation of is another term that means "against" the law.

IT'S ILLEGAL FOR YOU TO NOT USE THE CROSSWALK WHEN YOU CROSS THE STREET!
STOP
HUH!
HRC
IT'S ALSO DANGEROUS!

Here are some wrongdoings regulated by our legal system:

- **Torts:** A tort is a wrongdoing that hurts another person or his or her property. A person who commits a tort is usually required by the court to pay some money to the person he or she has offended.
- **Crimes:** A crime is a wrongdoing against a specific law that can bring harm to an entire society. Crimes vary in their degrees of seriousness. They fall into these three categories:
  1. **Infractions:** An infraction is a minor violation of the law.
  2. **Misdemeanors:** A misdemeanor is a violation of the law that is more serious than an infraction but not as serious as a felony.
  3. **Felonies:** A felony is a very serious crime for which a person might be put in prison for one year or more. In some states a person who commits a felony can be punished by death.

It is possible for an act to be both a crime and a tort.

I WONDER IF TYING DOG EARS IS A FELONY!

Torts and crimes can be committed by ***accident,*** meaning through ignorance or carelessness, or unintentionally.

SCREEECH!
BOP
OHHH!
I THINK A TORT IS ABOUT TO HAPPEN!

Torts and crimes can also be committed through ***negligence,*** meaning that one knows what is right but fails to do it.

THE BOY WAS RIDING HIS BIKE ACROSS THE STREET WHEN THE LIGHT WAS RED!
UGH!
IT'S A CRIME TO BE NEGLIGENT!

Torts and crimes can be committed through ***recklessness,*** meaning that one intentionally goes against what he or she knows to be right. When people commit torts or crimes, they are usually ***liable*** for their actions. This means that they are responsible for their actions and must suffer some consequences for their wrongdoing.

YOU KIDS MUST KNOW WHAT YOU'RE DOING IS WRONG!
GULP!

There are many kinds of torts, but not all of them are likely to involve you.

Some of the torts that might involve you are:

- invasion of privacy
- slander and libel
- trespass
- personal injury
- traffic accidents

...AND IT'S DEFINITELY A TORT TO GRAFFITI A DOG.

Invasion of privacy is, among other things, watching another person without his or her knowing about it or wanting it.

HEE HEE
UGH.
SPYiNG IS AN INVASION OF PRiVACY!

Slander and libel is a term that means harming another person's reputation by saying damaging things about the person. Slander is verbal. Libel is printed. The things that are said are usually false or unfair.

THAT ROBBIE IS A DIRTY LIAR AND A CHEAT!
THAT'S NOT TRUE!

Trespass is going onto another person's property without his or her permission or a legitimate reason to do so.

KEEP OUT
NO TRESPA
VIOLATO
WILL B
PROSECU
JETS
"BECAUSE I WANT TO" IS NOT A LEGITIMATE REASON TO TRESPASS!
GRAPES

Personal injury is harming another person mentally or physically. ***Assault*** and ***battery*** are two types of personal injury. ***Assault*** is a violent, verbal attack or threat. ***Battery*** is beating or using force on a person. If the assault or battery causes serious injury, it may be treated as a crime.

I'M GOING TO BREAK YOUR FACE, DOG BREATH!
TH-WOMP
...UMPH!
DID SOME-ONE ASK FOR A SALTED BATTERY?

Traffic accidents are accidents involving vehicles or pedestrians on public roadways.

When you walk, you are a ***pedestrian***, and you must

- walk where walking is permitted (on sidewalks, in crosswalks, and within designated areas);
- follow all traffic signals and signs;
- use crosswalks to cross the street except where there are none (then you must cross the street at the corner).

I DON'T HAVE TO FOLLOW TRAFFIC RULES! HUMPH!
OOOH... I CAN'T BEAR TO LOOK!

If you fail to do any of these things and your failure causes an accident, you have committed a tort.

BY NOT FOLLOWING THE TRAFFIC SAFETY RULES, YOU CAUSED THAT ACCIDENT!
YOU ALSO COMMITTED A TORT!
STOP

When you ride a bike, you must

- equip it as required by law;
- ride with the traffic on the right-hand side of the street;
- not drive carelessly or overload your bike with passengers or packages;

HEY, HEY, LOOK! NO HANDS!
FRAGILE
GLASS
CHINA HANDLE WITH CARE
NO BRAINS.

- signal when you are about to turn or stop;
- follow all traffic signals, signs, and pavement markings;
- obey all other traffic laws.

If you fail to do any of these things and your failure causes an accident, you have committed a tort.

BY NOT OBEYING THE TRAFFIC SIGNALS, YOU'VE COMMITTED ANOTHER TORT.
YOU'D BETTER OBEY THE LAW OR YOU'LL NEVER GET THROUGH THIS BOOK ALIVE!

If you have committed a tort, you are responsible for your actions and must suffer the consequences of your wrongdoing.

The court might order you to pay for damages if you commit the following torts:

- invasion of privacy
- slander and libel
- trespass
- personal injury
- traffic accidents

A tort that causes serious injury can be treated as a crime.

NO TRESPASSING
DO YOU BOYS KNOW THAT YOU ARE BREAKING THE LAW BY TRESPASSING ON THIS PROPERTY?

As a child, the only time you are not personally responsible for committing a tort is when an adult's encouragement or negligence causes you to commit a tort.

OUR PARENTS SAID WE COULD GO FISHING HERE!
THEN I'LL HAVE TO TALK TO YOUR PARENTS BECAUSE THEY ARE RESPONSIBLE FOR YOUR BREAKING THE LAW.
NO TRESPASSING
CAN WE STILL KEEP OUR FISH?

If someone commits a tort against you, it is your right to ***sue for damages.*** This means that through either a court decision or settlement, the person who harmed you can be required to pay for whatever damage he or she did.

The court decides whether the person will have to pay and if so, how much. Of course, you should have your parents help you with this. Your parents might decide to get legal help. If the court decides you deserve to be paid for the damage done to you, the money that is paid belongs to you.

IT IS THE RULING OF THIS COURT TO AWARD THE PLAINTIFF A SETTLEMENT IN THE SUM OF $100 FOR DAMAGES TO HER BIKE.
THIS IS BETTER THAN "TV COURT"!

A ***crime*** is a wrongdoing that can bring harm to the entire society.

Crimes are against the law.

There are many kinds of crimes, but not all of them are likely to be committed by children.

Some of the crimes that children might commit are:

- arson
- vandalism
- conversion
- larceny
- burglary
- robbery

Arson is purposely setting fire to a building or other property.

ERBIRDS
I'LL TEACH THOSE THUNDERBIRDS NOT TO LET ME IN THEIR CLUB! I'LL BURN DOWN THEIR CLUBHOUSE!
UGH!
GAS
ARSON

Vandalism is willfully or maliciously damaging or destroying public or private property.

Conversion is taking another person's property, using it without his or her permission, and then returning it.

THERE'S JIM'S NEW BIKE. I THINK I'LL TAKE IT FOR A WHILE. HE'LL NEVER KNOW THE DIFFERENCE!
HEE HEE
DON'T YOU WANT ME TO ASK JIM FIRST?
CONVERSION

Larceny is stealing. It is taking another person's property with the intention of depriving him or her of it permanently.

SWIPE
NEW
PiG Peopl
I'M NO PiG!
HELP! HELP!
HEY! THAT KID IS STEALING!
LARCENY

Burglary is breaking into and entering a building or place with the intent to steal something.

I HOPE HE'S A CAT BURGLAR AND NOT A DOG BURGLAR!
BURGLARY

Robbery is the act of taking something from someone by force or violence.

HUMPH! YOU LITTLE POTATO HEAD.
KA-THOMP
BARK BARK
THAT'S DOG LINGO FOR HELP!
HEY! THAT'S MY SKATE-BOARD!
ROBBERY

Other crimes that might involve children are:

- **kidnapping** (seizing or holding a person by force)
- **rape** (sexual intercourse with a person against the person's will or by force or deceit)
- **murder** (the deliberate and unlawful killing of a person)

Although these crimes are seldom committed by children, they are sometimes committed against children.

HELP! I'M BEING KIDNAPPED!
UGH!

Although hitchhiking is not always against the law, it can be extremely dangerous and can possibly lead to your being kidnapped, raped, or murdered. For your own protection, you should not hitchhike.

LET'S HITCHHIKE!
ARE YOU NUTS? NO WAY! IT'S TOO DANGEROUS!
VINE
MAPLE
THIS KID'S BRAIN IS ABOUT AS BRIGHT AS A BURNED-OUT LIGHT BULB!

To help keep you from being involved in crimes, communities have made ***loitering*** and being out after ***curfew*** illegal.

Loitering is standing around idly in public places. It is against the law for you to loiter.

NO PARKING
SORRY, GUYS. BUT HANGING AROUND IS THE SAME AS LOITERING.

Curfew is a fixed time at night when you must be home. Actual curfew times vary from community to community. Being out after curfew is against the law.

WE'D BETTER START HOME IF WE'RE GOING TO MAKE CURFEW.
YEAH!
WHAT TIME IS IT? MY WATCH STOPPED.

Many of the laws that relate to you have been established to protect you.

Some of these laws have been established to protect you ***physically.***

HEY MAC!
I WANT TO BUY SOME CIGARETTES!
I'M SORRY, BUT I CAN'T SELL CIGARETTES TO ANYONE UNDER EIGHTEEN.
HOW ABOUT BEEF JERKY?

Because it has been proven that smoking tobacco can be harmful to a person's health, it is against the law for an adult to give or sell you tobacco (such as cigarettes or cigars). In some states it is against the law for you to smoke in certain public places.

COUGH
HACK
COUGH COUGH
BOY, THAT SURE LOOKS LIKE FUN!

Because it has been proven that the misuse of alcoholic beverages can be harmful to a person's health, it is against the law for an adult to give or sell alcoholic beverages to you. In some states it is against the law for you to drink or possess alcoholic beverages in certain public places.

LIQUORS
DRAT.
WELL, WHERE ARE WE GOING TO GET SOME BEER?
You MUST be 21 to purchase alcoholic beverages.
HOW ABOUT SOME ROOT BEER?
JET

Because it has been proven that the misuse of drugs can be harmful to your health, it is against the law for you to possess, use, or furnish any other person with illegal drugs.

PSSST... WANT TO TAKE A TRIP?
NO! USING DRUGS IS AGAINST THE LAW!
HRC
YOU KEEP THAT UP AND YOU'LL TAKE A TRIP... TO JAIL!

Some laws have been established to protect you ***mentally*** and ***morally.***

Therefore, it is against the law for adults to provide you with pornographic material (pictures or writings that show erotic behavior and are intended to cause sexual excitement).

CAN I BUY ONE OF THESE?
IT'S AGAINST THE LAW FOR ME TO SELL YOU THOSE! SORRY!
NUDE
GIRLS
LOLA COLA
BOOK OF

It is also against the law for you to see movies rated X.

RATED X
DRAT!
LOLA COLA
LOLA COLA
I'D RATHER SEE LASSIE!

According to the law, you may not go into places that have been designated "for adults only."

In addition, adults may not sexually abuse you.

- ***Sexual molestation*** is making unwanted sexual advances.
- ***Rape*** is having sexual intercourse with a person against the person's will or by force or deceit.

Sexual molestation and rape are against the law.

HE'S AN ADULT. I'M SUPPOSED TO OBEY ADULTS. IF I DON'T DO WHAT HE SAYS, HE COULD HURT ME!
GULP!
UGH!

Some laws have been established to protect you ***in your relationships with others.***

The law protects you from your own unwise decisions by allowing you to change your mind in a business deal. Therefore, according to the law, you may void (cancel) a contract (agreement) you have made.

This means that if you agree to do something, you can change your mind. The fact that you can void a contract also means that if you buy something and decide to return it, the person who sold you the item must refund your money.

MARKET
99¢
$3.26
CAN I GET MY MONEY BACK ON THIS BONE?
19¢

Being able to void a contract also means that if you sell something to someone and then want it back, the person who bought the item must give it back to you if you return his or her money.

The law protects you from being hurt by making unwise agreements. Although this is true, this does not mean that you should make decisions carelessly.

YOU WANT TO BUY MY USED SKATEBOARD?
HMMM, I'D BETTER THINK THIS OVER CAREFULLY!
HRC
HAVE YOU ANY USED FRISBEES FOR SALE?

If you want people to trust and respect you, you must be a person who is worthy of trust and respect. This means that you should never enter into a contract or agreement with another person unless you intend to keep your part of the deal.

NO THANKS. I'D RATHER NOT BUY A USED SKATEBOARD.
HRC
NO FRISBEE, NO DEAL.

The laws that you have learned about in this book have been established so that you and the people around you can lead safe, productive lives. For this reason . . .

IT IS IMPORTANT THAT YOU UNDERSTAND AND OBEY ALL THE LAWS THAT RELATE TO YOU AND YOUR COMMUNITY.
SO YOU DON'T BECOME A JAiL BiRD!
OH, BROTHER.